ISBN 978-0-9935755-2-5

Edited by Rhoda Molife, MolahMedia

Printed by Catford Print Centre

To Hatta.

Families together
London.

Doing a fantastic job

Well Done.

Smart x

Ray x

Robyn Smart was born and bred in Brixton, South London. As a child, she was an avid reader and spent most of her spare time in the local library. She even started writing short stories at the age of 8.

As an adult, though armed with a law degree, she was compelled to return to her first love, writing, and in 2015, self-published her first book, 'My Magic Scarf.'

With her 2nd book, 'Who Am I?' Robyn shows her unique ability to write about everyday issues with remarkable insight into family dynamics, depth, aptitude and humour. She fully articulates the emotions of her characters using a rhythmical writing style that is engaging and entertaining, drawing inspiration from her experiences and encounters in the vibrant South London community.

Email: roby.smart@hotmail.com

Facebook:
https://www.facebook.com/RobynSmart13/

Twitter: @RobSmart13

WHO AM I?

BY

ROBYN SMART

I looked in the mirror

And what did I see

An ugly face looking at me

My eyes looked so big

Gazing, staring intently

I wish I could look more like

My friend Kimberley

**But what did she say when I
told her my fears**

'Girl, love who you are and
just wipe those tears'

I examine my hair

All nappy and hard

Doesn't even go straight

Not even with lard

My nose is so wide

Big enough to slide

Like a funfair ride

But what did she say when I
told her my fears

'Girl, love who you are and
just wipe those tears'

My complexion is different

From the rest of my friends

But if I cleanse

Like the advert says

Then maybe just maybe

I will transcend

Into someone more acceptable

Someone who is loveable

But what did she say when I told her my fears

'Girl, love who you are and just wipe those tears'

My lips are so huge

Protruding and vast

Now I'm beginning to think

Just get a mask

To cover this face, that I hate

But it's too late

But what did she say when I
told her my fears

'Girl, love who you are and
just wipe those tears'

My arms are so dangly

My legs are too lanky

Oh gosh I just dislike my
body

No one will like me just as I
am

I need to have a plan

To change who I am

But what did she say when I
told her my fears

'Girl, love who you are and
just wipe those tears'

Turning around to the left

To see more in the mirror

I can see

That I need

To lose some weight

But if I stood up straight

Pulled everything in

No, no, that makes me look

Like a piece of string

But what did she say when I
told her my fears

'Girl love who you are and
just wipe those tears'

I'm just too tall or am I just
short

I feel like a liquorice allsort

I'm skinny, I'm round

I need to lose a few pounds

Gain a few

What would you do?

I'm dark, I'm fair

And please don't mention

The hair

I just need to find who I am
Just be myself

Love me for me

And nobody else

But what did she say when I
told her my fears

'Girl, love who you are and
just wipe those tears'

Chapter 1

Melanie lifted the magazine which had been idly left on the dining room table. On the front cover shone a beautiful model whose hair was shiny blonde and swept neatly across her face, showing just a hint of the carefully applied makeup.

Lifting the magazine to the light, Melanie attempted to see whether there were any spots lurking on the model's face, or even just a blemish. The magazine rose higher and higher until it nearly caught alight on the lamp above. Nope, no blemishes, no spots, no pimples - nothing, nothing at all. Just plain peachy skin with rosy cheeks and a neck any giraffe would be envious of.

Melanie had questioned herself time and time again. 'Why did models always have that stark look about them?' One that made them look like they had just watched a horror movie. Dressed in a mint green outfit, the model stood in front of a black horse which somewhat overshadowed her elfin-like body. At the most she was a size 6-8, no more than that. So, is this the criteria for a model then? Peachy, light insipid skin, coupled with a dainty and fragile waif-like body? Melanie had a lot to aspire to.

Over the next page was another model, wearing sunglasses which did not do her face justice at all. Seemingly three sizes too big, the rim was a dark rustic colour with the rest a light oyster, highlighting her face, which was pale, almost ashen.

Melanie could hear her sister playing music upstairs. It was just too loud and the lyrics to the song made Melanie cringe;

some of the things being said were void of morals and totally improper.

Focusing her attention back to the magazine, a page caught Melanie's eye: a page crowded with models sporting army clothing from top to toe. Melanie particularly liked a khaki pair of trousers, with a slim waistband and which were flared at the bottom. Her heart began to race slightly as at last she could see something that could possibly fit her, but as she checked the details it was only available in small sizes. This was ridiculous.

At 14, I had developed into a portly, tubby, or some would say, podgy teenager. How I didn't know. I remember my mother one day saying to me, "Mels," this was her pet name for me.

"Mels, you're going to have to stop sneaking into the kitchen and eating all the biscuits. I mean look at your sister, she's in proportion to her size, just neat in all the right places. You however, well you could do with losing a few pounds."

'In which places exactly was she neat?' I thought. Neat meant spotless, immaculate or ship-shape. I didn't think my sister was any of these. Helena was my older twin. Older by 36 seconds to be precise, and she always thought she had the upper hand in everything.

At this point Helena and her music were giving me a headache. On top of that, she wasn't getting into trouble for it. That's the part that got my goat the worst. Reaching for my headphones, I continued to peruse through the magazine, scrutinising every page, scanning over the models and their attire. Realising that the army trousers would never fit me I turned the page over. Extra firm hold spray. Long lasting leaving your hair manageable.

"Hell, no, not my hair," I whispered under my breath.

It was only a few weeks ago I had begged, absolutely begged my mother to relax my hair. For those of you that don't know what it means to 'relax' hair - it's a method of applying chemicals to your hair to loosen the kinky curls, straightening it and giving it the appearance of European hair. Oh, how I longed for that look.

Every morning I struggled and tugged with my hair. On my dressing table lay a horde of broken combs. Some smashed, others cracked, one or two fragmented. And, why you may ask? Well, because of this damn nappy hair I had. Nothing would work with my hair. Mum tried everything - wax for nappy hair, pomade for nappy hair, sheen for nappy hair. To be honest there was nothing on the market for a girl with nappy hair so I had to settle with mixing a touch of hair gel with water, smoothing it into my hair, and then tapering it down on my head with a scarf. This at least gave my hair a nice wavy look. But hell, if it rained I was in trouble.

I remember what happened some time ago after a game of netball. I played centre. That position was such hard work, having to manoeuvre yourself all over the pitch defending every corner. As the match ended, I could see dark clouds gathering above. That only meant one thing for me. Hurry the hell up, get ready and get home! But oh no, my sister had other ideas. You see Helena did not have the same problem as I did.

Although we were twins, her hair was as straight as an arrow. No kink, no stray hairs. Just straight. Now both of us knew people questioned the fact that we were twins. Helena was so fair, she could pass as mixed-raced, meaning of mixed heritage - white and black. But, in our case, this was definitely not true. We both had the same parents but the differences, especially as twins, were stark. My brother Adrian used the word 'blatant'. Yes he was right, there was no ambiguity here. However, based on our features, you could see, just about, that we were related in one way or another. People often commented on our voices saying we sounded alike, especially over the phone. But when people saw us it was a completely different ball game.

Anyway, on this day, I hurried off the pitch just as soon as the shrill of the whistle blew and handshakes were exchanged. In a flash, I was in the changing room collecting my things getting ready to go. But...Helena, in usual

Helena style, was laughing loudly, giggling and sniggering at one girl who had fallen a few times during the match. My sister had an evil, malicious streak in her, one which really annoyed me.

I was waiting patiently at the gate for her as she continued to mock and make fun of the girl. At that point a few raindrops fell. Becoming restless at having to wait, I began to walk slowly out of the gate towards the graveyard which was adjacent to the school. As I got closer to the main road, the rain became heavier. This only meant one thing for me: SHAME AND EMBARRASSMENT. Turning around to see where my sister was, I saw her walking at a snail's pace, lingering with her friends.

Parked on the corner was a large jeep so I leaned forward peering into the side mirror and saw the hair disaster begin to unravel.

Leaning forward I touched the top of my head which was now saturated. To add injury to insult, there was someone sitting in the car. I jumped back quickly almost tripping as I did so.

My hair began to kink and what was earlier a neat style was turning into what looked like a lump of gunk, all white round the edges morphing me into a freak. Feeling as though I was about to wet myself, in my mind, I begged my sister to hurry up. Surely as my twin she would sense that I really had to get home fast!

Sure enough, she lifted herself from a loud belly laugh and saw the look of fear and anxiety on my face. Making her excuses to her friends she ran to catch up with me, flipping her umbrella up to protect what was left of my dishevelled hair.

"Why did you wait?! You should have just walked up!" she exclaimed.

"No I couldn't do that, remember Mum said we should always walk home together when the evenings got dark. You should have just hurried up."

The rest of the journey continued in silence with slivers of hair gel dripping onto my nose. Oh, yes the nose...

Chapter 2

Well my nose was the butt of all the jokes in the family. If anyone wanted to really wind me up, they just had to go for my nose. It wasn't that it was big as such, just wide and spread across my face, more than any other nose in the family. It kind of had a life of its own. If you met me, I guarantee that once you got past my hair, the next thing that would get your attention would be my nose. But where did this nose come from?

One day whilst the house was deserted, I scoured the house for the stash of photo albums which had been hidden in a trunk in my parents' room. Opening the door, I could smell the lingering scent of Mum's expensive perfume. Dad had bought it for her on Mother's Day, obviously pretending it was from us. Foraging under the stash of unused pillows and covers I located the albums. The first one I came across was Mum and Dad's wedding album, protected by its original plastic cover which must have been all of 20 years old.

That's how long Mum and Dad had been married. I always wondered how anyone could stay together for such a long time. They seemed to get on each other's nerves, but nonetheless acted as though they were lifetime companions. Dad said you need to know the game: just nod and smile and say yes to whatever Mum says. He said that was the recipe for a good marriage. No doubt some people would disagree.

I tentatively opened the album and the first picture that greeted me was one of Mum and Dad climbing into their wedding car. Mum looked adorable in her white lace wedding dress. In fact, on this day without a doubt, she looked like a model. Dad was sleek in what looked like a made-to-measure suit. But this was my Dad all the time. As a manager, he always wore a suit except at the weekends, when he conformed more to an urban style of dress.

Hearing a noise, I jumped, but it was only the cat, Muzzy. She knew she wasn't allowed upstairs but always tried her luck. Seeing the door open and the house quiet was too much of a temptation for her not to snoop around. After shooing her out, I flicked though the album quickly, just trying to get a glimpse of anyone that remotely looked like me. There must be someone, at least one person. Grandma or Granddad, Auntie or Uncle? Someone.

As I got to the last page but one, I gazed at a shot of at least 50 people in a group photo. My eyes scoured quickly, combing each face for clues. Hmm... considering this was 20 years ago everyone was dressed quite dapper. The women had carefully applied makeup all matching their skin tones, with shades of eye shadow to match their clothing. As I immersed myself in the intricacies and details of their attire, I realised that I had drifted from my original venture.

And then...at that point...I spotted a lady - tall, well not tall, but definitely not short, who kind of looked like me. The eyebrows were shaped like mine. Her forehead was shaped like mine. With her smile, I could see she had dimples like mine. But, most of all, yes most of all, she had the nose. That distinct broad nose. Noticeable and markedly just like mine. I breathed a sigh of relief. At last, someone like me.

At one point in my life I actually had started to think that I may have been adopted and that the 'twins' thing' was a lie made up to make me feel wanted. So this might be proof that I was wrong. I ran to my brother's room where his mobile phone lay on his dressing table already charged. Grabbing the phone quickly I ran back into my parent's room. I had to take a picture.

As I tried to zoom the phone camera in, the image seemed to blur. This made the lady's nose look even bigger than it was. In fact, it began to look distorted. While fiddling with the phone I heard voices outside. I had to get this picture now, because I was actually in forbidden territory.

When Helena and I were younger we once went into our parents' room to play. As we pried, we came across what we thought was the best find ever - the largest box of chocolates we'd ever seen. We both looked at each other, giggled and delved into the massive box, chomping hard on each one and then grabbing frantically for the next. A few minutes into our escapade our antics began to backfire. I started to feel a rumbling feeling in my tummy and looked up to see Helena grasping hers. Something was seriously wrong. Then, 'poop' - one came out, then 'poop' – two, then – 'poops' in unison, then 'poops' in chorus, and then a whole fraternity of 'poops' erupted from the both of us. We began laughing hysterically but the more we laughed the more the 'poops' came out. But then the 'poops' turned into runny...well you know what I mean and before we knew it we were surrounded by what I could only describe as a sea of runny...

Unbeknownst to us, the prized box contained diet chocolates that Mum had been using to help her lose weight...something she was always trying to do. If you ate too much they gave you, yes you guessed, the 'poops' and the runs. So, we both sat there on the bed, rigid, not able to move until our parents returned home. They could smell the mess as they opened the door, and as you can imagine they were livid. Everything had to go - sheets, pillows - even the mattress had to be dumped. From then on, we were banned from our parents' room unless they were there.

But today was an exception because I had to get this photo. What I was going to do with it I didn't know, but I had to have it. I heard voices, and as they grew louder, the camera clicked. In my haste I had taken it. My palms were now sweating but I still had to get a second photo. Click. Done. The voices then floated through the front door.

I grabbed all the bedding and pillows that I had tossed onto the bed and threw them back into the trunk. Smoothing down the bedcovers, I made a speedy exit to the bathroom.

"Melanie, are you up there?!" shouted Dad.

"Yes Dad! In the bathroom, just washing my hands."

"Ok. Where's your sister?" he asked.

"She's next door with Betty," I replied.

"Fine. We got pizza. Come down when you're ready."

Phew! Was that a close shave or what?! With the phone stuffed down my top I had to move carefully so as not to let it drop into the toilet when I had flushed it, as I had to pretend I had used the toilet. My brother would kill me if that happened. Tiptoeing across the landing, I made my way to my bedroom where I carefully emailed the photo to myself. Then after deleting the picture from my brother's phone, I sneaked it back into his room. Now I had the evidence, but what would I do with it? Well at least I had it and I could make up my mind about that later. Walking triumphantly down the stairs, I began for once to feel a sense of pride, a sense of belonging. My family didn't know how totally isolated I felt on some days. My inner thoughts detached me from everyone else in the family. I looked different, I felt different and in my solitary moments of despair, I separated myself from everyone else. But today none of those feelings were present. I felt victorious in my find and so I was now going to eat a celebratory slice of pizza... or two!

Chapter 3

I dived into my pizza and as I was about to help myself to another 2 slices I could see my mother watching me out of the corner of her eye. I sunk back into my seat and decided to go for a bowl of the salad, 1 hot wing and a piece of garlic bread. Mum smiled slyly, nodding her head in approval without saying a word.

"Hey Mel, you not taking another piece of the pizza? There's plenty to go around," Dad said.

"No I'm fine Dad this will do me."

"Yes," Mum interjected, "Mel knows she needs to watch her weight."

"Weight, sleight," Dad retorted, "she's only young, and she'll grow out of it. Puppy fat, just puppy fat!"

I loved it when Dad stuck up for me, although I knew better than to have any more pizza. My mother's wrath was not worth it. Mum hastily left the kitchen remembering she had to call my aunt - something about a new diet they were starting together. The subject of weight in our family was paramount, well, except for me. Her exit was the perfect excuse to ask my Dad if he thought my nose was big.

"So Dad, do you think my nose is really big? I'm always being teased about it and nobody else in the family has a nose this size." I should have been prepared for the narrative he was about to bestow upon me. Dad was big on long explanations. This one though would change my perception of my nose forever.

Chapter 4

"There was a French philosopher and historian called Constantine De Volney who was very angry about slavery. He had always thought that the ancient Egyptians were white.

However, whilst visiting Egypt, he was totally amazed to learn that they were not white but black, and that the sphinx's facial features were those typical of Negroes (black people), especially the lips and most notably the nose. It was said that since Napoleon did not want people to know that the Egyptians were of African descent, their noses were shot off with cannonballs."

"That's the short version," Dad said. "If you want the long version, get on the internet."

Totally bemused and intrigued at the same time by what Dad had said, I asked, "So should I be proud of my nose then?"

"Oh without a doubt my sweetheart. Women out there are getting their noses done just to look like you. And for the record your nose is distinguished, not big."

Plucking up the courage to show him the picture, now that I had him on side, I walked over to a kitchen drawer where my phone was kept during school time. This was to be sure that it didn't distract me from my work. I sat down and clicked onto the email with the picture that I had taken.

"Dad, can I ask you who this is?"

"Hey! Where did you get that picture? Have you been snooping? Your mother will kill you! Let me have a look?" he replied. "Yes that's Big Nose Berta. I mean Auntie Berta, and she's your grandma's sister, your grand-aunt. Oh, I see where you are going with this! Yes, I see the likeness."

Just as Dad continued to nod his head in agreement, Mum entered the room, looking as if she'd won the lottery.

"So it's agreed - the diet starts on Wednesday, yeah," Mum said. "And, what are you nodding your head about mister?" she continued. Dad quickly shoved the phone into my hand, "Oh just Melanie's homework. I was agreeing with her on her use of similes."

In my head I wanted to laugh but bit down hard on my lip to contain myself. Holding my countenance and leaning onto the worktop I waited for Mum to tell us about this new diet. To be honest though, I wasn't interested. Just as she was about to delve into the gritty details, Helena made her appearance. There was something different about her, but at first glance I couldn't make out what it was. As she came closer I could see that she had highlighted her hair. A pang of jealousy gave me a spasm in my stomach which made me hiccup.

Dad called her nearer and Mum's face had a noticeable frown. "What in God's name have you done to your hair?!" Dad bellowed.

"Hush Frederick hush, no need to shout so loudly." Mum held onto Dad's arm trying to placate him. She knew that Dad would need pacifying with this one. Helena looked frightened, but as usual, she had an answer for her misdemeanours.

"Betty's older sister is an apprentice at a hair salon and wanted to try me out with some streaks. I think it looks cool."

Even I had to admit that it did look good. It made my sister look older and most of all even more European.

So now we looked even less like family. I looked like the poor sad black girl and she looked like the hip white chick. Without saying a word, I left the room feeling even worse about myself than I had ever felt before. I went up to my bedroom and behind me could hear the excitement in Mum's voice and the simmering of Dad's. So, they had accepted it.

Laying on my bed, I reached for the magazine I had been looking at a few days earlier. Page 15. A lady buys a cashmere jumper just so people could stroke her. My, people were desperate for attention these days. Why would you want strangers touching you just because of your clothes? Maybe it's me who has the issues. I did have issues. I was jealous of my sister. Her features, her hair and the fact that she got away with almost everything she did. Lowering my head into my pillow I began to cry. I sobbed and I sobbed until I didn't even realise that my bedroom door had been opened. It was my brother. I sat up and wiped my face, snot dripping from my big old nose onto my jug lips as they quivered.

"Hey, what's up? What's with the tears?"

I was so upset I couldn't respond, my big lips sealed together as if stuck with superglue. I then found my voice.

"Oh it's nothing. I'm fine, really I am."

"Sure you are. Wipe your face. You're making yourself look even uglier than you are."

Only my brother could get away with this and we both laughed.

"Chin up sis you're beautiful really."

I leapt from my side of the bed which was sunken because I had beaten it so hard with hate. Not the bed's fault.

"You think so? Really?"

"Of course. Ever read the ugly duckling?"

Strange that my brother was trying to make me feel better but had mentioned 'ugly' at least twice. Contradictory as it sounded, he was making me feel good though. With that said he left my room and I stood looking in the mirror at my ugly face.

Later that night my sister swanned into the bedroom singing at the top of her voice. "Do you mind? I'm trying to read!" I shouted.

"Read? You don't read a magazine, you browse through it. With all those adverts there's barely anything **to** read. Hold on I don't recall you saying anything nice about my hair?"

"I didn't get a chance, but it does look really nice." I said it and I meant it.

Chapter 5

So, it was now becoming apparent who the most beautiful sister was, and Helena did not feel any remorse about showing off about it. To top things off, with a wedding looming, Mum decided to take us both shopping for outfits. Man, was I dreading this. Long gone were the days that we were dressed alike as if we were two black china dolls. People would stop our parents at the shopping centre cooing over how cute we were. Now some 14 years later we couldn't be any more different.

The morning of the shopping trip arrived and as usual Helena was the first up, dressed and ready wearing a pair of cut jeans, matching jean top with hair tied back and hoop earrings. I, on the other hand, was wearing a track suit with my baseball hat as I was having a bad hair day. Today gel refused to slick back the hair, so my hat camouflaged it nicely and neatly.

We waited patiently for Mum to get herself together. She always took forever, whatever the occasion. I remember hearing Dad once tell her off as she put on her best trainers, embossed in diamanté, with matching tracksuit, to go, where you may ask? The dump? Right! I could hear Dad's shouting, asking her where in the hell she thought she was going.

Today as she came down the stairs, I could see she was wearing a twin set top and cardigan in a coral colour with a matching skirt bordered with white lace. I wondered if she realised we were only going to the local shopping centre. She was dressed as though she was going to a work meeting.

Some years ago, we attended a festival where some 'freak,' as Dad had labelled her, colour-matched my Mum to her personality. I remembered waiting well over an hour for this lady to print a report that would correlate Mum's celestial and spiritual colours with her personality. Since then, Mum invested in every colour similar to coral which apparently was *her* colour. My Dad insisted it was a load of poppycock. However with her now adorning herself in everything coral, she did get a load of attention and compliments. Maybe that's why Dad tried to divert her from wearing *her* colours and join him in his dull and dismal greys and blacks. BORING.

Climbing into the car I could see my sister looking at me out of the corner of her eye. She did this quite often which wound me up. If you are going to say something then just spit it out - don't just stare at me. Most of the time I already felt like an oddity, a mutant of some kind, and staring at me just made it worse.

"What, are you looking at?" I asked as I took my position in the car. My sister paused before she answered.

"Um it's just that the hat doesn't sit right on your head, and it certainly doesn't match what you're wearing."

Angrily I retorted back, "And I care because? We are going shopping, not to a fashion parade."

"It's just that it looks kind of strange. Why won't it flatten down more on your head?"

With that my sister reached over and tried to push my hat further onto my head. But with it being a hair disaster day, it wouldn't budge. The more she tried to wedge it down, the angrier I became. When she used both hands to try to secure it further, the anger in me welled up.

"Will you get your scrawny hands off my head, and leave my damn hat alone?!"

As the words tumbled out of my lips I knew I was going to be in trouble.

"Melanie Rachel Monique Louisa Mitchell that is enough! Enough! And then you children wonder why I have to pay so much car insurance - it's for lack of concentration when driving with two teenagers arguing about rubbish!"

After hesitating, I eyeballed my mother in her rear-view mirror. Why oh why whenever I got into trouble, did my mother have to call out my whole government name, *and*, who in their right mind would give anyone four names anyway? Furthermore, who started this nonsense?! Again, Helena got away with it. She always did. I shuffled myself away from her but my large bottom was stuck. I moved left then tried to shuffle myself to the right but there was no give. I was pinned in the spot next to the trouble maker.

As we pulled into the car park, I knew we would be here for at least another 15 minutes. Talented as she was, parking was not one of my mother's strengths, and so we had to drive around looking for the largest bay possible. Considering she drove a very small car, one would not believe the shenanigans she got entangled in when trying to park. I set the timer on my phone to see how long it would take her to secure a suitable parking spot. Just like clockwork, as the last digit turned to 0 down from 15, the engine was turned off and the ticket secured on the windscreen.

Helena and I got out of the car from opposite sides. Whilst Mum was leaving the car, Helena waited patiently to hold onto her arm as usual, like a lost child. I stepped out in front of them – I didn't have time for this. Catching sight of myself in the shop window, I was taken aback by my reflection. Yes, my sister was right. My hat looked a bit strange, or maybe I only thought it did because she had mentioned it. This was the problem. In myself I felt content, at times even happy with who I was. Then I would see a photo in a magazine, a woman on the television or my sister would make a comment and I'd feel inadequate and defective in some way.

Moving closer to the window just to double check my appearance, I decided to take off the hat which I thought would make me look better. Not realising how close I was to the window – BANG - I knocked my face against the glass, slap in the middle of my forehead.

I felt dizzy. I felt disorientated. I thought I'd broken the glass. Panic overwhelmed me and after blinking a few times realising I was still conscious, I spun around to hear both Mum and Helena laughing at me. Not one of them asked if was ok, or how it had happened. They just laughed and laughed. They only stopped when the shopkeeper came rushing out to see how I was, already equipped with a towel and ice.

At this point, they realised the seriousness of the situation. Helena continued to snigger though, but Mum caught herself and had stopped - more so out of embarrassment than concern. She began to fuss grabbing the ice from the shopkeeper's hand and pressing it firmly against my forehead. She pressed so hard that I thought she would leave a large dent. In fact, I'm surprised that there wasn't a gaping big whole on my forehead. Boy oh boy was I in pain!

By this time a small crowd had gathered adding to the embarrassment of the whole thing. Mum pretended as though she was deeply concerned.

"Oh my darling how did this happen? I'm so sorry!" she wailed.

The shop keeper explained that he had to go and left us with the ice. Soon after, the crowd dispersed. It was only then that I saw my sister not only still giggling but making gestures with her hand. Still feeling dizzy, I couldn't make out what she was doing, but slowly I realised she was pretending that she had a bump on her forehead.

I turned around to look back into the window to see if I could see the Mount Carolina forming on my head.

"Oh no you don't young lady! We are not having that again," said my mother. Mum decided to abandon the shopping trip and get me back home to rest.

"YESSSS!!" I shouted.

I looked at Helena's face and she was devastated. It was now my time to laugh.

Chapter 6

Arriving home after what seemed like an eternity, I lifted myself out of the car. During the drive I had felt dizzy and sick. Mum said I must have had a slight concussion. There was nothing slight about how I felt though. We entered the front door with Helena dragging her feet behind her, making it clearly obvious that she was fully peeved about not being able to fulfil her favourite pastime of shopping.

Dad had his head buried in the newspaper. He loved having Saturdays to himself going through his papers, page by page, as if it were a shopping catalogue. First he'd go through the news section, then the finance section, then the holiday section, then the home magazine, then the fashion section. Everything. Page by page. He raised his head slightly but didn't see me holding a large towel against my head.

"You girls home early - shops on strike?" he chortled. "Staff must have seen the 3 of you coming and shut the doors."

I wasn't sure if he thought he was funny. We did have a reputation for spending the whole day, and sometimes a night, at the shops, but today certainly wasn't one of those days. Mum shifted her weight slightly to the left. I could see from her body language that she was nervous about telling my Dad about my little accident. You see though I was prone to accidents, they always happened when I was out with Mum and never with Dad. Once, she lost me in the shopping centre. Another time we were at the park and I fell off the swings. Not Mum's fault but...

The last time we went shopping, she was in such a hurry to get me out of the store that we walked out with an item that still had a security tag on it. She had walked out before me and I still had the bag, with the tagged piece of clothing, which set the alarm off. So the security guards came running towards me whilst she had already swanned off.

It wasn't until 10 minutes or so later that she realised I wasn't in tow. She traced her steps back to the shop to find me in a back room with one very kind police officer and the security guard. She fumbled in her purse to find the receipt and it was only until then was I let go. In the meantime, I had had visions of spending the night in a cell, with the walls closing in on me, as I lay on an uncomfortable bed, looking at the ceiling, awaiting my fate. Just like those jail scenes shown on TV.

When we got home, the whole story was grossly exaggerated. It went from a tag being left on one item of clothing, to a whole load of clothes with tags on, and from there being one security guard to a police van arriving at the shopping centre. Boy did my Mum know how to embroider the truth and embellish a story. I wasn't sure why she did this though.

Anyway, back to the present. As my Dad realised that there was silence, he slowly lifted his head from the newspaper. There I stood in front of him with the biggest lump on my head ever. It protruded out like an alien probe. I stood feeling helpless, wanting to cry, but held it down for fear of looking even more stupid. My thoughts began to drift to how at this very point, I was even less attractive than my sister. Even if it was only an accident, it was one that left me feeling even more inadequate than I had ever felt before. As I floated into a day dream, the pain hit me as hard as the original collision. Opening my eyes from the daydream, I saw Dad's large hand hovering over my forehead.

He shouted at my mother who prior to this hadn't really taken the whole thing seriously. She sure did now though.

"How in hell's name did you let this happen?"

"What do you mean *I* let this happen?! The girl was so busy looking at herself in the shop front that she crashed into the glass! How that is my fault only God knows!"

I could sense an argument ensuing so decided to jump in.

"Dad, it wasn't Mum's fault at all. She's right. It was me. I wasn't happy about how I looked and tried to fix my hair not realising how close the shop window was."

Dad continued to frown, held my arm and gently led me upstairs to the bathroom. Opening the cabinet, he shuffled bottles around. Inside this cabinet was old and new. There were medicines that had expired some 3 years ago. Others were in multiples. Why did we need 4 identical boxes of paracetamol and 5 of Nurofen? All lined up like soldiers.

Watching Dad's face intently, I couldn't figure out what he was looking for. He moved several bottles and finally retrieved a brownish looking one. In large writing, I could see the words *Hamamelis Water* written on the bottle. These were 2 words I was familiar with ever since I was a young child. Hamamelis was part of the family and especially important for me. You see, as the clumsy child, I was always getting myself into scrapes ending up with bumps and bruises. When this happened, out came the trusted old Hamamelis Water. To some, it was known as witch hazel, a plant used by the Native American Indians. It's often used as an astringent for cuts and bruises, bumps and scrapes, so was made just for me.

Before I knew it, Dad had soaked a large piece of cotton wool with the liquid. He then applied it to my forehead. It was cool and soothing. He held the cotton wool in place for what seemed like forever, then began applying pressure which made me yelp like an injured animal trapped in the woods. Just at that point my brother flew into the bathroom, swinging the door so hard that it nearly hit Dad in the face. I could see another accident happening here, and we would have needed 2 balls of Hamamelis-soaked cotton wool then. Dad swerved out of the way of the door which then jolted his hand which applied even more pressure to my head. He was angry.

"What do you want in here?! This is none of your business! Go and tidy that tip which you profess to be a bedroom. I will be coming in there in 20 minutes, and anything still left on the floor will be put in the bin as you already seem to think your floor is a bin."

"OK Pops. Chill. I'm nearly there, just a few more bits to do. By the way Melanie, I hear they are doing auditions for a new alien movie. You should try out." He ran out of the bathroom sniggering. Dad slowly moved his hand away but I dared not look into the mirror.

"Now that's better!" Dad exclaimed.

I knew I could trust Dad so I slowly turned around towards the mirror and could see a marked reduction in the size of the bump. I breathed a sigh of relief. He suggested that I took 2 paracetamol tablets from the mountain of boxes in the cabinet. After he had brought something up for me to eat, I was to rest. This made me feel even better because I could get away from being in the limelight, away from the family staring at me.

Chapter 7

The next morning I woke up with a banging headache. It felt as though I had done 10 rounds in a boxing match with a world heavyweight. I knew the difference between heavyweights, lightweights and bantamweights because my Dad, when not reading newspapers, was well into his boxing.

Adorning the living room walls were framed photos of famous boxers, from Lonny Liston to the great Mohammed Ali, who had recently died leaving my father distraught. He had even thought about going to America for the funeral, but Mum persuaded him otherwise, saying it would be better for him to watch it on the big screen in the living room. And a big screen it was. It was a massive 55-inch with surround sound, high definition and a curved screen.

What I loved about it was because it was in high definition, I could see all the flaws in the characters on screen, and that made me feel a lot better about myself. Recently, whilst watching a movie, I was sure that the wrinkles on one lady's face looked like the lines on the tube map. There were so many stretching across from one corner of her face to the other. In fact, if you looked closely some resembled a whole road.

If there was one thing I could say, it was that at least my skin was flawless. I was blessed with that. As a teenager, I didn't have any spots, not one, well maybe one or two, but not like some of the girls in my class. One girl was constantly teased and other students called her 'Motley Spotty Susan.' Her face was covered, absolutely covered. I felt sorry for her. Most of the time she just looked as though she wanted to run and hide. When anyone met her for the first time, they would just stare.

A knock on the door jolted me from my thoughts and my head began to throb even more. I lowered my sore head into my hands, as I heard the trudging of feet enter my bedroom. I lifted my head gently to see my Dad's slender frame blocking the doorway holding my favourite cup. I knew straight away he had brought me a cup of frothy hot chocolate. I didn't think this was the best time of the day for hot chocolate, but if it soothed my headache, then I'd have it.

Dad spoke in a gentle tone. "Melanie, I've got something for you." As I lifted my head higher the pain seemed to intensify. It was now concentrated in my neck and down my spine. How could a small bang cause so much pain? As my Dad handed me the cup, I could see that in his other hand was a box of more paracetamol tablets alongside a plate of toast. Pulling myself gently up the bed, I reached out gratefully for the cup and plate.

"So my poppet, how you feeling this morning?"

I steadied myself in the bed.

"Well, not so bad, but my head still hurts. I'm sure these tablets will help and a bit more rest."

Dad sat on the edge of the bed.

"Mmm...not so sure about rest because the shopping trip which was planned for yesterday has not been totally abandoned. In fact, the other 2 are getting ready as we speak."

"Oh you've got to be joking me," I retorted. "I still don't feel good and I'm sure I've still got a bump on my head. I probably look like Quasimodo."

I lifted my free hand to feel where the lump had developed and to my surprise it had disappeared. However, I felt disappointed because I didn't feel like traipsing around the shopping centre.

"Dad, do I really have to go? I mean shopping, not the wedding. Couldn't I just get something online?"

My Dad looked at me, confused. "Online?! Are you joking? You'd never find anything to fit you online!"

As the words came out of his mouth I could see that he'd realised he had said the wrong thing. Trying to retract his statement, he began to stutter.

"What I mean is that they wouldn't have anything that would suit you. I mean both you and I know you have very high standards and your taste in clothes is just like your mother's. Stylish and fashionable and chic. Not like Helena. She has no clue about elegance and sophistication. She's just happy to put on any old thing."

Both he and I knew this was a lie. He was only saying this to placate me, but it was too late. Having searched the internet myself, I knew that trying to get into some of the outfits there just would not work. I *had* to try everything on.

Thinking about the hours ahead with Mum and Helena filled me with dread. I hadn't done anything with my hair. I hadn't plaited it or put a scarf on it so it would be a challenge to manage now. I wanted to shout at the top of my voice, 'I'M NOT COMING, LEAVE ME ALONE!' But that would not have gone down too well with Dad.

As it was a Sunday, the shops didn't open until 11 which gave me an hour and a half to get ready. One thing that persuaded me to go was that Dad said he would be coming. Gosh that was so unusual. Dad said he hated shopping like a dose of poison. I often wondered when had he actually taken a dose of poison, and if so how did he live to tell the tale? I think he must have been speaking metaphorically.

Dad said that shopping with women was the worst thing any man could put himself through. He often commented at the number of arguments he could count as we drifted from shop to shop. How many men were sat in corners with piles of bags bulging at the seams? Dad would comment, 'Start at shop number 1 then circle around to shop number 10, only to go back to shop number 1 to get what they originally wanted. What a waste of time and energy.'

So why was he coming today? I was miffed. As I walked out of the bathroom, I caught my Dad coming out of the bedroom brushing his hair. He had such silky hair. It needed very little attention and I didn't often see him brush it. You see, my Grandad, my father's father, was Jamaican and of mixed race. His mother was from the parish of St Elizabeth and his father was a general in the British Army.

Apparently when the ships docked the soldiers would go to visit the local women for food and parties and spend time with them until it was time to go back to sea. Despite this I wasn't blessed with hair from my father's side of the family. Instead I got my hair from my mother's side, the side with the nappiest hair ever. All of them either relaxed their hair, or had protective styles so you never really saw their hair type. The only protection I ever had was my baseball hat or bedtime scarf.

"So Dad, why are you coming shopping? Are you going to buy yourself some clothes as well?"

He looked over the top of the bannister, moved a few steps, opened his bedroom door, and then looked over his shoulder. Right about now, he looked like a spy. I stood still, bemused by his movements. In a hushed lowered tone he said, "No, I'm coming to keep an eye out for you and make sure you don't have any more accidents. But mostly to make sure you get something you like and are not coerced into buying something the others like."

As the last word left his lips, my Mum appeared from my brother's room.

"That boy's room is a tip, clothes on the floor, food on the floor, games on the floor. Anyone would think I gave birth to him on the floor."

Why would my mother give birth on the floor? She baffled me sometimes and what was even more baffling was that she hadn't even asked how I was, how I felt, or how my head was. I made my way to my bedroom turning slightly to see my Dad covering his lips with his fingers, and my Mum marching down the stairs still complaining.

I then heard her say loudly, "Oh Helena you look gorgeous. How did you get your hair to stay up like that? I just love the bun." My heart sank as I closed my bedroom door quietly and sat tentatively at my dressing table glaring at the pile of broken combs.

Chapter 8

Sluggishly I got up and made my way down the stairs. I could already hear the flurry of the others making their way to the car. I was more confident about going because Dad would be there. I waited at the top of the stairs until everyone had climbed into the car. Thank God Dad was driving. That would avoid the nonsense of Mum taking 10 years to park. Mum plopped herself in the passenger seat and glanced out the window. I wasn't sure if she was looking for me or if she even cared whether I was coming or not.

Dad tooted the horn several times which was his alarm to say 'come on, let's get going.' I walked down the stairs and made my way to the front door, pausing slightly to put on my new trainers. Because my feet were quite wide I struggled to get the trainers on. I sat at the bottom of the stairs, pulling the laces, tugging hard, but still couldn't get my feet in. 'What's going on?' I thought in my head. 'My feet must be swollen. Oh this is ridiculous!' As I became more frantic I heard the horn toot twice. Having travelled enough times with Dad, I knew that one more toot would mean keys in the ignition, engine on and car off, with whoever was or wasn't in the car.

I remembered a time when we were all meant to be going out for a family picnic and Dad, in usual Dad fashion, was ready on time. My brother had woken up late as he usually did and we waited and waited for him to get ready. Because Mum knew that my brother had no sense of urgency whatsoever, she told him that the trip was an hour earlier than it actually was. So we were meant to leave at 11am though she had told him 10am. Despite this, my brother was still running late. Everybody was already packed in the car including a hamper filled with fried chicken, rice, homemade coleslaw, homemade ginger beer and sorrel, all of which my Dad really loved. We waited and we waited and we waited.

In fact, we had waited so long that the car windows had steamed up. I wrote **hurry up bro** on the window and yet he was still nowhere to be seen. At that point, my Dad tooted the warnings, 4 toots, then 3, then 2 and then as he was about to toot once, both Helena and myself looked at each other. We knew that meant we were about to go. Dad banged the horn aggressively because he was so angry at having to wait. The sound of the horn sounded like thunder clapping in the sky. We were all anxious. You could see beads of sweat dripping down Mum's face because she had really put a lot of effort into planning this family day out. But Dad was adamant.

"No, no," he said, "that boy needs to learn how to get ready on time. I am fed up of him taking his time, thinking that the whole world waits for him. Well it doesn't! What is going to happen when he starts working? Does he think that the workplace will wait for him to turn up an hour late every day? I don't think so. No, we need to teach him!"

So with that, the engine roared as my Dad pressed the clutch, pushed the handbrake down, put his foot onto the accelerator, and indicating left, slowly set off. My heart was pounding so much. Pounding because whenever we did have family days out, I kind of got on with my brother more than I did with my sister. She felt that she was too, I don't know, posh to mess around. Whereas my brother and I, well, we'd just let loose and enjoy ourselves. Whether it was water fights, chasing each other, or playing rounders, we just seemed to have that connection that allowed us to laugh and have fun. So for me, this wasn't just a case of my brother not coming and him being upset when he saw that the car had gone, but also about the fact that my day would be just plain boring.

Jumping out of my daydream, I realised now that both trainers were securely on my feet with the laces tied perfectly. I pulled the door behind me and could see the others in the car. My sister was in her normal position spread out across the back, and as usual I prepared myself to battle for space to sit comfortably.

"Okay, take a deep breath," I said to myself.

I slowly opened the car door and she seemed to move over a little bit. I tell you, if there was one thing to be said, it was that when Dad came out with us, there was no messing around from my sister at all. I think she was kind of scared of him. Not that he hit us or anything. It was the look he'd give us when we stepped out of line. One that meant all manner of things including 'wait until you get home.' It was glaring, penetrating even, and it was all he needed to do. Anyway I got into the car, she moved across and I was able to sit down and for once sit comfortably.

"So," Dad said, "all the ladies in my life in the car. Let's go. And oh, by the way, I'm only planning to spend a few hours out with you guys. I've got things to do myself this afternoon and I really don't anticipate being out all day looking for frocks."

"Frocks?!" my Mum said laughing. "Who uses the word frocks nowadays? That's so old school. It's not frocks darling, but dresses, you know...dresses."

Dad glanced out of the corners of his eyes. He knew what he was saying, he was just trying to make things a little light-hearted so that it would take away the tension in the air.

As we drew closer to the shopping centre, my heart started to flutter. I recalled the shenanigans of yesterday. Even though the lump on my forehead had gone down, I still had intermittent headaches though I didn't tell my Mum or Dad. The headaches were still a reminder of what had happened. How embarrassing it all had been. I didn't even think I could walk past that shop again. What if the shopkeeper came out of the shop and recognised me? Oh my God, what would I do? I could put my head down and pretend as if it wasn't me. Then again, if I was with Mum and Helena then he would know that it was me. I wondered if we could just not go past that shop.

The car pulled into the car park. Dad was a dab hand at parking. All he had to do was find a space, and by looking in the rear view and the side mirrors he'd reverse in straight away. And today he did just that. We all left the car and I decided to grab onto my Dad's arm. It was something I'd

74

always done as a child. It made me feel secure and comforted in some way. Helena held onto Mum's arm as always. It was like we were separate teams but still a family, though sometimes it didn't feel that way.

Walking towards the shopping centre, I could tell that Dad was becoming more agitated. He pulled his jumper down and then rolled the sleeves up. Not that his sleeves needed rolling up. You could tell he was just doing it because of the tense atmosphere. So we all marched through the shopping centre, the family moving together, no one really looking at each other. I for one felt really uncomfortable, but being with Dad gave me that feeling of security. But who's to say nothing would happen, knowing how clumsy I was.

The first shop we approached was quite a fashionable one. Mum and Helena always went in there. I hated it. Why? Because, yes you guessed it, nothing there could fit me. So whilst they were trying things on, I would be sitting on the uncomfortable square puffees with no backs, but still having to lean backwards, swinging my legs from side to side, wondering whether anything would fit me. On the odd occasion, I would catch a glimpse of myself in the mirror before swiftly turning back around because I really didn't want to see my ugly face.

Yes. You heard me. I did say my ugly face. Quite often I couldn't look in the mirror. When we were out in public, I would try to retreat into a corner whilst the other two giggled, trying on different dresses which always fitted them, whilst I was left out as usual.

But this time as we entered the shop Mum was not holding Helena's hand. She began to hold onto my arm which came as a surprise to me. Actually this was very strange, and I didn't know what to make of her gesture. I took it in my stride as best as I could though, as we moved towards a clothing rail which didn't look too bad.

Moving the hangers along and grating them against the pole, we looked at the different sizes and colours which all looked quite nice. But as I gradually looked up I realised we were looking at the plus size rail. Is that what I was now? Was that what all the gentle hand holding was about, soothingly leading me to this? Size 14 was hardly plus size, was it?

Why my mother had brought me over here only God knows. My confidence plummeted again as I realised this is how she saw me. I mean I was podgy, a bit chunky in places, but I did not see myself in the territory of *plus size*. After all, Dad said it was puppy fat. I circled around to see if he was conscious of the fact that we were at the plus size rail, but he was nonchalant, even blasé about the whole situation. He just coolly observed other women trying on clothes with their husbands or partners commenting as they excitedly bustled in and out of the changing rooms.

I was upset that he wasn't concentrating on what was happening right in front of his eyes. It really did upset me. I felt like kicking over the rail and walking right out of the shop, until I caught sight of a dress which I thought didn't look too bad. So, I swallowed my pride and picked it out. Both Mum and I looked at each other and she smiled with glee. The excitement began to build up from the pit of my stomach hoping that at last I had found something. However, we then realised that the dress had been hung on the wrong hanger and was actually a size 6. Just as I was about to put it back, I felt Helena's breath on the nape of my neck. 'Here we go,' I thought.

"Oh look," she exclaimed loudly, "that's soooo nice! Hey Mum do you think it will fit me? Just look at those colours. They look like Kente colours. Do you know what I mean by Kente Mum?"

Mum retorted back, "Yes Helena I do know what you mean and yes I think it would suit you. Go and try it on."

As Helena walked towards the changing room, Mum called her back as she saw something else that would fit her. They both then headed towards the changing room sniggering, leaving me in the middle of the shop like billy no mates. Meanwhile Dad's attention was waning rapidly, as he was already making his way out of the shop.

So, I was left on my own. I walked around and looked to the left where they had other dresses that might have been a good fit, but the colours were disgusting. As I continued to circle around the area an assistant appeared from nowhere frightening me out of my skin.

"Hello young lady. Can I help you at all?"

I wanted to reply, 'Do you have clothes for fat cows? Yes, fat cows with udders.' But the words didn't reach my lips. That's how I felt right now though – like a fat cow.

"Uh, no, I'm fine thank you," I responded. "I'm just waiting for my sister and my mother - they are in the changing rooms."

"Oh yes I've just seen them and they look absolutely stunning in that top of the range stock."

A lump came to my throat. I felt as though I was about to choke. I didn't want to look at them. It wasn't long before the pair, yes the pair, emerged from the changing rooms and of course I had to take a peek. Mum looked fantastic. The dress accentuated her figure and suited her tone and Helena looked stunning. I swallowed hard and bent down pretending to tie my laces again. As I did so I could hear the conversation between them.

"Oh Helena we are going to be the talk of the wedding. People will be looking at us," Mum said.

Yes. She was right. Staring at them and not me. Talking about them and not me. Looking at me for the wrong reasons, and at them for the right reasons. I fiddled around with my laces until I could no longer take it. The tears trickled down my cheeks and I then began to cry heavily, with tears now saturating the front of my new trainers leaving stains as they fell, one after the other.

I tried to pull myself together as I could hear them approaching rapidly, excited to show me how they looked. But I had no tissues and there was bogey everywhere. I tried to sniff up as much as I could, but that didn't work. In fact it made me choke, which drew attention to me. In desperation, I turned around to see a dark green cardigan on a rail right next to me, and yes, you guessed it...I pulled the sleeve of the cardigan close to my face pretending as though I was feeling the material and ever so diplomatically wiped the remnants of bogey onto the sleeve. Yes I know it was disgusting but there wasn't anything else I could do. I wasn't about to wipe it on my sleeve, was I? I looked up and for one split second it appeared that they had realised I had been crying. But I was mistaken, they didn't understand my feelings. In fact, they didn't care about my feelings at all, just about themselves.

I stayed silent for a few minutes, feeling the nasal drip drain down the back of my throat hoping that the tears in my eyes would dry up. With all the enthusiasm I could muster, I whispered, "You guys look nice - the dresses suit you. At least you have something that fits right?" Before they could answer, I heard my Dad's dulcet tones behind me.

"Hi there ladies. Aren't we looking good?" He then realised I was still sitting there with no outfit, nothing to try on, nothing that fit, nothing that suited me, just nothing for me. I saw his expression change.

"So Mels, where's your dress? Where's your outfit?"

"Oh I didn't see anything that suited me and the clothes in here are just not my style."

"Surely there must be something in here that you like?"

"Well, actually, there isn't, and this is only the first shop. I don't have to get anything in here do I, or do we have to go home now?"

You could see my Dad was torn about which way to answer. Ideally he would have liked to have an early escape.

"No Melanie, I don't mind, but there must be something in here," he said.

In a firmer tone I responded, "No Dad, there isn't. I want to go somewhere else."

"Oh well, it's your choice. Let's go and pay for these dresses. By the way how much are they?" As I thought about what I was going to buy, I heard my Dad shout, "How much..."

Chapter 9

By now we were on the 5th shop. Shops 2 to 4 didn't have anything that suited or even fitted me for that matter. This was becoming a chore. So here we were, at shop number 5, rapidly running out of choices. In desperation, Mum came up with a suggestion: my aunt could sew me something. I started thinking that the idea could work, except, knowing my aunt well, it would take her 15 years to finish making something.

Once, when I was 7 years old, Helena and I were both meant to go to a fancy dress party. Year after year at school we would have to dress up for World Book Day. But this year, after our car had broken down 3 times, Mum decided that enough was enough. She was no longer going to pay out for any more fancy dress costumes.

So, she drafted in the skills of one of our aunts who was a seamstress in her day.

Following several phone calls and a number of visits for measuring up and chats about colours and designs, my aunt proceeded to make our costumes. The night before they were to be delivered came the phone call.

"Oh hi, it's Auntie Mavis. Unfortunately, there has been a problem with my sewing machine. The needle broke and I only managed to get one costume made, the one for Helena as it took up less material and time because you know, she's a lot skinnier than Melanie. Not quite sure what you're going to do." Overhearing the conversation from the next room I was horrified. Did that mean that I wasn't going to have a costume at all? I heard Mum's response.

"Oh don't worry, I'm sure we will find something for Melanie. She can probably wear one of the old outfits from my wardrobe. It really isn't a big problem."

I can wear something from my Mum's wardrobe? Was this some kind of joke? At the age of 7, I could hardly fit into my Mum's clothes. What on earth would I be doing wearing a woman's clothes to a kids' fancy dress party? I was depressed, a depressed 7-year-old. But on the day of the fancy dress party, Mum decided to dress me up as a character from Charlie and the Chocolate Factory. In fact, I didn't look too bad. It was just that the clothes were slightly baggy.

I now knew I didn't want my aunt to sew me a dress, so I was determined to find myself something to wear. Dad pulled out the stops to help me in my quest. The other two were not interested at all and proceeded to start looking at jewellery and shoes that would match their dresses. Dad and I walked around slowly in a methodical fashion on a mission to find something.

As I glanced over to the far corner near the changing rooms, I glimpsed a suit. I took a deep breath and beckoned him over quietly so that the others could not see it before he did. So he walked over tentatively. I was excited, and felt butterflies in my stomach. Checks needed to be done first. Right size tick. Right colour tick. I spun the outfit around then pinned it against me daring to look into the mirror which stood to my left. I didn't pay much notice of my top half. It was the area that the suit covered that concerned me most. So the last check was making sure that it fit. I picked up another outfit I had seen and liked, just as a backup. The assistant came over to help and advised that there were several others but in different colours I could try on. We walked hurriedly over to the stand to pick them out. The anticipation was killing me. I began to feel elated. I entered the changing room on a high, floating, with the 3 outfits in my hand. I looked in the mirror and what I did see was my nappy hair gazing at me. No. Forget that for now and just try the dresses on. I calmly set about undressing and in my mind I secretly prayed:

Dear Lord,

You know how difficult it is for me

I'm struggling with who I am

I don't know who I am

The others just laugh

But please just for today

Make at least one outfit fit

Please God

I'll finish my homework on Wednesday

And won't blow my nose in another

Cardigan.

As I was praying and dressing I noticed the ripples of fat on my stomach. I need to go to the gym. Actually am I even old enough to go to the gym? Hoping it didn't get stuck, I tugged at the skirt and eventually it fell into place. Done. Ok. I reached out for the top slowly, pulling it over my head so as to not mess up my hair, even though it was already a mess. Slipping my arms into the sleeves, everything was now in place. Spinning around with my eyes closed I summoned up the courage to open them and there I saw, for once, a beautiful me. I smiled.

It wasn't often that I used beautiful and me in the same sentence, but today I did. I pretended that my hair didn't exist and concentrated on everything else. The smile turned into a grin, the grin into a chuckle, the chuckle into a happy little laugh. I was definitely happy. I looked at myself from all angles in the 3-way mirrors, pulling them this way and that, and was simply delighted with what I saw. I wanted to sing really loudly but contained myself. I tried on all 3 outfits. Let them wait. I was happy in my moment of splendour.

When I finally left the changing rooms I tried to hide the outfits from Mum and Helena. I had decided that I didn't want them to see anything I had bought until the day of the wedding. I called Dad over and he asked what the damage was. In comparison to the others mine were quite cheap so he decided to get me all 3 outfits. Reaching for his leather-bound wallet, he went for the black card and winked at me as he punched the pin number in the card machine. I gently punched the air. I threw my arms around my Dad's neck. He was embarrassed as he wasn't one for public displays of affection. But I could see from his grin that he too was pleased.

Chapter 10

On the ride home I was floating on cloud 9. The grin on my face spanned from ear to ear. Both Mum and Helena looked at me in bemusement. Maybe they thought I was going crazy. I'd leave them guessing. They hadn't seen the outfits and wouldn't do so until the day of the wedding. I even had choices. When did I ever have choices? I was always so restricted, until today.

Before I knew it we had pulled into our road. Suddenly though, Dad broke sharply. We all jolted forward as he narrowly missed a black cat crossing the road in its own sweet time. Luckily I had my seatbelt on. Hmm...a black cat. Good omen or bad omen? Well for me it felt like a good day. Dad composed himself and moved slowly forward to locate a parking space right outside the house. This was a rarity, to find a space outside our house. Hmm...as I said, it was a good day.

We all got out of the car wearily, especially Dad. It had been a long morning for him traipsing around with 3 women, well 2 teenage girls and 1 woman, for clothes. Dad grabbed the bags from the boot but I clung on to mine for dear life. I could not take the chance of anything happening to my clothes. As Mum fiddled with the door keys, like she always did, we could hear the shrill of the house phone from the hallway.

No one was in a hurry to get it as in our household we didn't really use our house phone much. So consumed by the technology of mobiles and free minutes, the house phone was now like an ornament perched on the table in the hallway. Each one looked at the other to see who would answer the call, and as Mum had nothing in her hands at all apart from her large bunch of keys, she picked up the receiver.

"Oh my baby Shakira!!! How are you? Where are you?" shrieked Mum.

I just realised I hadn't mentioned Shakira. Shakira was the other sister. The eldest child. The only one who seemed to have her head screwed on the right way round. Not only did she love herself, she was also always full of confidence and was appreciated and respected by anyone that met her.

Chapter 11

Shakira was 20, so 6 years older than Helena and I. But she seemed so much older. Having left school with very little in the way of qualifications, she had decided that she didn't want to go down the traditional route of university or college, but instead set up her own business. This at the age of 16. My parents were livid. Three generations had gone down the time-honoured route of heading off for a degree. One cousin had even gone to Oxford.

But my sister decided she wanted to be an entrepreneur and that being in a world of academics was not going to help her. Both Mum and Dad tried their utmost best to change her mind, but they could see it was a waste of time. So from that point on, they encouraged her in her pursuit of setting up her own company. When she was younger, my big sister worked for an estate agent on Saturdays, helping with viewings and carrying out the administrative tasks. Since then, she developed a liking for the business of buying, selling or renting properties. In fact, she loved anything to do with the business. As the years passed, she decided to work as an ambassador for rich clients who wanted to buy homes. Her role was to hunt for suitable properties for them because they didn't have the time or patience to do the legwork themselves. Soon, Shakira had not only built up an extensive portfolio of clients in England but soon gained a reputation for her services.

People from all over the world sought her out and this led to her travelling to all sorts of countries. She was now in Dubai. How I longed to be able to visit different countries like that. How I would I didn't know, as I was scared of heights and planes made me feel sick. So I suppose that whatever I wanted to do had to be in this country unless I overcame my fears.

I could hear Mum's voice rising with glee.

"You're coming home?! When?! I'm so excited! For the wedding? That will be brilliant! Ok my darling. I will tell your Dad and the other 3 and we will see you in 2 weeks."

Hearing the news cheered me up. I always loved when my sister came back home, least of all because she always brought me back something nice. Sometimes it was even clothes...that actually fit.

Shakira didn't get on that much with Helena. She said she was too superficial. I didn't even know what that meant until she broke it down for me. "Someone that's shallow sis, kind of phoney, not real."

"How can someone not be real?" I had asked her.

"Well they don't know or like themselves so they put on a false personality, a front. Half the time people can see through it though."

This was deep. I put up a front most of the time. Pretended as if I was happy and content with myself and how I looked, but only Shakira knew the truth. She knew me inside out. She took the time to know me. We spoke a lot. Mostly by text or sometimes skype. She lifted my dark moods.

"Sis, love who you are. Don't let anyone put you down. Always have confidence in yourself. Have courage and strength of character."

The things she said were always a lot to take in but I tried my best. Once she told me that when I walked, I should walk upright, chest out, bottom in. So one morning after feeling particularly lifted by her divine words I decided to follow what she said, right down to the last letter. Shoulders back. How would I get my shoulders back? Ok. So I tried rolling my shoulders as far back as I could, stuck my chest out, a chest that was quite big for my age and squeezed my bottom in as far as I could. God, I felt uncomfortable. When I reached the bus stop a little old lady tapped me on the shoulder to ask if I was ok, and that if I needed a toilet I could use hers as she lived right by the bus stop. I must have made it look as if I was busting to go. What a sight! I abandoned that one.

The next bit of advice she gave me was, 'When you shake someone's hand, always keep good eye contact and have a firm handshake.' I knew I would try this one out when I went for any interviews. There were none lined up though, but I'd always remembered what she said. So, basically, my sister Shakira was my mentor.

Helena tapped me on the shoulder, shaking me out of my thoughts. What did she want now? I suddenly felt my happy mood go sour.

"So little sis, you not going to show me what you bought then? Don't think I can't see you hugging your bag."

With one fell swoop, Helena attempted to snatch the bag out of my clutches, but I was one step ahead of her and tightened my grasp the moment she began to speak. It was a good thing the carrier bag was thick or else all would have been revealed. Snarling at her I responded, "None of your damn business so leave me alone!"

I think she was surprised at my response and lessened her grip. More so because she heard Dad's voice coming up behind her. Swiftly making my way up the stairs I felt my heart pumping. There was nothing as hard as keeping a secret, so I knew it wasn't going to be easy. I looked in my

bedroom scanning each corner to see where
I could hide the bag.

Chapter 12

The countdown to the wedding began and the house was abuzz with excitement. Dad and my brother had even made a day trip to the shops to get matching suits for themselves. Boy, did they look smart when they tried them on. We all felt proud. However, before this, each day after I had come home from school, I could see that someone had been rummaging in my room. I wasn't sure if Helena had paid Mum to do so because she was usually the only one at home before we got in. Gosh this was so funny! But between you and me, having told my Dad about my fear of the others seeing my outfits, he kindly took them to work for me and hid them in his locker. So whoever was ferreting around my room wouldn't find anything.

I lay on my bed contemplating how I would look at the wedding. I imagined how for once people would be looking at me and saying how good I looked. It was then that it hit me. **MY HAIR.** What would I do with my hair? The panic swept over me like a tsunami and the tidal wave of emotion enveloped me as I realised that I had no plan in place for my hair. I quickly ran downstairs to grab the laptop but couldn't find the charger plug. Why was it that when there was an emergency I couldn't find the charger?

The laptop was a communal one. Not a great idea because it always meant that whoever was the last to use it would have left either their unsaved work on, or would have deleted your unsaved work. Whilst scouting for the charger I decided to add to my Christmas list:

1. **Laptop of my own...not to share.**

There was no harm in asking.

As I finished scribbling my wish, I saw the charger poking out from underneath the dining room table. Elated, I dived to grab it but as I did. I slipped and banged my leg on the table. While writhing in agony and trying not to cry, the front door opened with Mum and Dad walking into the hallway.

Bemused at seeing me underneath the table rolling around, Dad asked, "Mels why are you adorning the carpet with your body? Don't tell me this is some new dance they are teaching you at school."

Through gritted teeth, mainly because of pain but also because of bewilderment as to how ridiculous his question was, I responded, "No Dad, I just tried to get the charger and tripped."

I didn't mention that I had dived. Just embroidered the truth a little bit. I saw his long thin arm reach under to give me a hand up and in doing so I nearly banged my head again. Soooo accident prone!

Standing up but still rubbing my leg, Mum dropped her shopping bags noticing I had a bruise.

"I think young lady you should put a warm compress on that now. You don't want a black bruise on your leg, do you?" Why did she say a **black** bruise? Why not just a bruise? Colour was such an issue in this family.

Hobbling up the stairs to the bathroom, I went to the magical cabinet and, yes, you guessed, grabbed the good old Hamamelis Water. I doused it on a towel and then wrapped the towel around my leg. This was such a waste of valuable time. I was meant to be researching hairstyles for natural hair. After rocking back and forth in pain for a few minutes my leg felt better.

Leaving the bathroom I bumped into Dad in the hallway, charger in hand.

"This will save you a trip downstairs as obviously you are eager to have it."

"Yes. Thank you Dad."

I fumbled in my pocket.

"Let's swap the charger for my Christmas list...well the first part of my list anyway."

Dad seemed anxious until he saw the list...of 1, and burst into laughter.

"Yes we'll see about that young lady."

Hopping into my bedroom I plugged in the laptop and waited for it to boot up. Gosh it always took so long. Once the logo came up telling me it was ready, I typed in 'natural hairstyles for girls.' Hmm...should I change 'girls' to 'teenagers?' I guess it didn't matter much as I just needed ideas. I wasn't hopeful but to my surprise a full

10 pages came up. I was thrilled to bits. Although my hair was natural, it was still quite long and so most of these styles would suit me. But the problem was, where would I get it done? The elation quickly turned to disheartenment. We knew loads of hairdressers that did relaxing and pressing and all of that. But who could do natural hair? I wondered if Shakira would know someone who could do something with this nappy hair.

I jumped up and made my way to the dressing table mirror. I loosened the two plaits which I had styled a few days ago, and had managed to keep neat by tying my headscarf securely each night. As my hair unravelled I could see that it had that kind of wavy or some might say kinky look. Either way, for once, I was pleased with it. I grabbed my phone quickly and searched anxiously for the camera button on the phone. Then I remembered I had to turn it around to take a selfie. I ended up taking a picture of myself in the mirror though.

I turned my head slightly to the left. I looked like a model. Now I was ready. I pressed the button and clicked once, twice, then 3 times. Spinning the phone round I searched in the gallery for the pictures. Wow! I was impressed. Totally impressed! I sighed a happy sigh. For once, I was excited about my hair. Then a plan came to mind. I would send the pictures to Shakira and she might be able to give me some ideas on how I could transform my hair and get a new look. Sprawling back onto my bed, I carefully typed in her email address. Then I wrote her an email:

Hi big sis. How are you? Hope all is good. I can't wait until you are here for the wedding. Can you believe that I found something to wear? Helena is begging me to see it but I've hidden it so she can't get her grubby hands on it. In fact, Dad bought 3 outfits. Maybe when you come you could help me choose which one looks the best if you have enough time. Anyway, the main reason for emailing you was about my hair. Yes, I hear you saying, not that old story. But it's still a story for me, an ongoing trilogy. Soooo, I think I may have found a hairstyle, and I'd like you to give me your thoughts and let me know how I can jazz it up for the wedding.

Mum and Helena have already made their hair appointments and can you believe they haven't even asked what I plan to do? Maybe they thought I was going to shave it all off (smiley face with teeth). I have attached the pictures to this email so let me know what you think.

Ps. Love you sis.

Just as I was about to press 'send,' there was a knock on my bedroom door. Searching wildly around the room for something to hide the screen, I located Puddles my baby teddy bear and turned the keyboard around.

"Come in."

There stood Helena in the doorway with a haughty look on her face. I think she was born with that look. She always seemed so self-assured, whereas I was always self-conscious. Seeing her standing there meant nothing but trouble.

Chapter 13

"Hi Mels. Are you using the laptop? Hold on. Are you sending an email? Let me see!"

With that she leaned forward trying to move Puddles out of the way. I grasped at my bear, protective of my lifelong friend.

"Mind your own business and why are you in my room anyway? Leave me alone."

"I just wanted to ask what you were wearing to the wedding."

"You know better than to ask me that. I've already told you, you will see me on the day. Just leave it at that. I don't know why you keep asking me. Are you afraid I'm going to look better than you?"

Helena clutched her stomach and laughed one of her biggest belly laughs ever. She rolled with her legs up in the air, then rolled over onto her side still grasping her stomach. At one point, she looked as though she was going to stop breathing. Her face grew red. Being lighter than I was, when embarrassed, her face would turn red. When she was upset, it turned red. And when she laughed like this, yes you guessed it, it turned red.

I waited patiently for her to stop her cackling, wishing she would hurry up so I could send my email. But no. She continued rolling around adding a snort every now and again. Eventually drawing her last laugh, she looked up and spat out the words.

"You... look better than me? You must be deluded. Have you been drinking fizzy drinks? That would never happen. Not in a million years. Please don't get yourself confused with who is the prettiest, most intelligent, and above all, the favourite around here."

The words shot through my heart like an arrow, piercing all of my being. Lowering my head, I could feel the tears pricking through my eyes, but I refused to cry. I didn't want her to see that she had caused so much pain, leaving me feeling like I would crumple into a ball and just basically die. How could my own sister say something so evil, so wretched? No one would ever think that we came from the same parents. The vindictiveness and unkindness that came from her mouth was the worst there could ever be. She rose from the bed still smirking, leaving me feeling wounded and saddened.

Chapter 14

The days leading up to the wedding flew by and before I knew it, my sister Shakira was home. Relief was an understatement. I felt I now had an ally, a confidante, someone I could share all my woes with. What woes could a 14-year-old have you may ask? Well, since Helena's tirade of abuse, I had stopped speaking to her. I was quite good at ignoring people. I had a way of shutting them right out if I needed to.

Mum once told me that when I was a little girl, she refused to let me play with a particular toy and I didn't speak for a week. That must have been a record. They were so concerned. But for me it was like having the ultimate power, with everyone worrying about me. They thought about taking me to a speech therapist, until one day I was offered a chocolate brownie and exclaimed, 'yum yum!' With that, the week of silence was broken.

But this time until that evil sister of mine apologised she would not get the benefit of hearing my voice again. Mum and Dad sensed the tension and asked every day what the problem was. Dad even threatened us by saying he would withdraw our pocket money if we didn't start speaking, but I totally refused. They weren't going to know what had happened.

I confided in Shakira who just confirmed that Helena had issues but why she had them, who knew. She said she was insecure and because of that thought that putting me down would make her feel better. I didn't understand all this psychological nonsense. Surely I wasn't meant to at my age. But Shakira said that this episode was grooming me for the future, whatever that meant. With that explanation, I began to feel sorry for Helena but did not show her as much. Right now I just needed to concentrate on my hair now that my big sister was here.

The day of the wedding arrived and you could feel the excitement in the air. It was as though it was Christmas. Dad decided to get out his old records, yes records, not CDs, and play them as we all got ourselves ready. Mum was especially happy as both she and Helena had got new hairstyles. And I must say they did look pretty. But of course I only told Mum she looked pretty, and not Helena.

Shakira, despite being busy, dedicated all morning to doing my hair. She was annoyed at the fact that no one had even thought about what my hair would look like. First, she washed and blow-dried it. Then she pulled out a large black leather bag which looked more like a suitcase, and from it she took out several hair products. She lined them up on my dressing table and I read each label. None of them said anything about being for nappy hair. I always thought that I needed products specifically for nappy hair.

Leaning back into the chair I felt so relaxed and comfortable in the hands of my sister. In fact, at this point she felt more like my mother. Because I was nervous about today I hadn't been sleeping well, so I found myself dozing off in the chair. Before I knew it I had fallen into a deep sleep.

Suddenly, feeling a tap on my shoulder, I jumped and knocked my knee on the dressing table. Raising my head up I realised that my hair was done. I looked so pretty. **Melanie and pretty?** At the same time? How was that possible? Not only had my sister given me the best hairstyle ever, she had also done my makeup. How did she do that with me in dreamland? Whichever way she had, I was over the moon. Spinning around in the chair, I grabbed my sister's neck and gave her the biggest kiss ever.

Wait until Helena sees me! I asked Shakira not to tell the others how she had pampered me and decided to get changed in the haven of my bedroom. Left alone I revelled in the new me. I must have looked in the mirror around 100 times. Slight exaggeration, but almost 100. My hair was entwined with intricate plaits and pulled up from the back with a sweeping fringe in the front.

I soon realised that time was moving quickly so I reached for my outfit which was now back in my wardrobe from Dad's office. And Helena still had no idea where it was. Dressing quickly, but ensuring I didn't displace my hair, I slipped my outfit on from the bottom up. Wow did I look fantastic! I had also hatched a plan. I wouldn't leave my room until everyone was in the van. The family had hired it so that there was enough space for all 6 of us to travel together comfortably.

I could hear dad shouting from downstairs. We all knew what that meant. Taking the last of my selfies, I waited until I heard the flurry of bodies rushing down the stairs. Ten, 9, 8, 7, 6, 5, 4, 3, 2, 1. Time for me to go. As I waltzed down the stairs I held my breath. My new-found confidence was fading a little as I didn't know what the reaction of the family would be, both at home and at the wedding. Reaching the last step, I heard someone behind me. I thought everyone was gone. My brother came rushing out of his room, bringing up the rear as usual.

"Wow, sis you look amazing! I mean really amazing," he said in awe.

I thought I was hearing things. As he caught up, he held out his arm for me to hold on to. I felt so special as I placed my arm through his. Walking together to the van, laughing at his silly jokes, we startled the rest of the family. As I climbed into the van, I could see Helena's mouth drop, literally drop, wide open. She couldn't say a word. Dad looked at me in the rear-view mirror and winked. That's all I needed, his reassurance. Mum smiled proudly. We drove to the wedding in silence. Shakira sat close by showing her support by rubbing my hand every so often.

Chapter 15

As we walked up to the church we could see all the family members, young and old, dressed to the hilt, looking sharp and smart. Some of the faces I recognised, others I didn't. We were introduced to so many people. The number of cousins was unbelievable.

With the church ceremony over and the reception looming, we were ushered to a nearby hall which was adorned with beautiful flowers and decorations. Soft music played in the background. Each family was seated on tables named after flowers. We sat on the daffodil table which was perfectly fine with me as it matched the colours of my outfit. There were name cards on the table and I was ecstatic to see that I was sitting between my dad and Shakira. For once Helena looked lost. She was no longer in the limelight. It was strange seeing her like this. She looked solemn and sad. Our eyes met across the table and she smiled briefly but I could not get those vile words out of my head.

I turned my head to see the bride and groom walking into the hall as their arrival was announced. The bride looked stunning in a sequinned and jewel-encrusted dress with a long train. As they were seated, family members were left to mingle and it was then I felt a heavy hand on my arm.

"So whose child is this?"

I didn't recognise the voice but as it became louder I managed to see the side of her face. I felt I knew her. She was an older lady, older than my Mum, dressed in a cobalt blue suit with matching hat. Dad piped up, "That's my daughter. In fact 1 of my daughters. I have, sorry, we have 3 now."

The lady moved fully into my view. I knew this woman, but where from I couldn't remember. And then I saw the nose. It was like looking at an older version of me. It was the lady from the photo album. My great-aunt Big Nose Bertha. But she was pretty. Despite the nose she was pretty. She moved closer and seemed to home in on my nose.

"Hold on. This one has my nose. We are truly family."

With a wry smile I actually felt proud to be part of such a large and diverse family.

The reception was now in full swing and the speeches were underway. As I looked around the room, I heard my name called from the stage. I froze in my chair.

"Would Melanie come up to the stage please?"

Me? Why? Oh gosh! I felt my face get hot and I didn't know what to say. Little did I know that Dad had nominated me to say something to the bride on behalf of our family. Somehow I managed to sum up the courage to get up to the stage and say a few words.

As I was about to step down, the bride stood up and commended me on my appearance. Walking back to my seat I held my head high. I was walking on air. I was so happy that I wanted to cry. I saw each member of my family looking at me with pride, even Helena. I think she now respected me for who I was.

Leaning back into my chair, I began daydreaming and the words Shakira had said to me some years ago began to resonate above the voices in the hall.

'Girl, love who you are and just wipe those tears.'

Today was my day to love me for me.
Happy with my body, happy with my hair,
happy with my being. I closed my eyes
and wiped away a tear.